FUN WITH TENOR BANJO

BY MEL BAY

CD CONTENTS*

1. Introduction & Positioning [1:03]
2. Tuning: Introduction [:18]
3. Tuning: Notes [1:05]
4. Positioning Pick & C Chord [:41]
5. Time Signatures: 4/4 Time [:18]
6. Time Signatures: 3/4 Time [:18]
7. Time Signatures: 2/4 Time & G7 Chord [:34]
8. The G7 Chord Exercise [:31]
9. Strum Exercise for 1st Song [:50]
10. Long, Long Ago [:41]
11. Down in the Valley [:45]
12. Skip to My Lou [:36]
13. Buffalo Gals [:36]
14. Oh, My Darling Clementine [:38]
15. The F Chord: 4/4 Time [:29]
16. The F Chord: 3/4 Time [:19]
17. The Blue Tail Fly [:38]
18. On Top of Old Smoky [:56]
19. The Marines Hymn [:54]
20. There is a Tavern in the Town [1:10]
21. The D7 Chord [:21]
22. The D7 Chord: 4/4 Time [:25]
23. The D7 Chord: 3/4 Time [:19]
24. The D7 Chord: 2/4 Time [:24]
25. Our Boys Will Shine Tonight [:35]
26. The G Chord: 4/4 Time [:30]
27. The G Chord: 4/4 Time [:26]
28. The Old Grey Mare [:43]
29. She'll Be Coming Round the Mountain [:31]
30. Hand Me Down My Walking Cane [:33]
31. Red River Valley [:42]
32. 3 New Chords [:18]
33. Fun With Chords in "C": 3/4 Time [:20]
34. Fun With Chords in "C": 4/4 Time [:21]
35. More Fun With Chords in "G": 3/4 Time [:23]
36. More Fun With Chords in "G": 4/4 Time [:22]
37. Home on the Range [1:08]
38. I've Been Working on the Railroad [1:01]
39. In the Evening by the Moonlight [:40]
40. The D Chord [:18]
41. The D Chord: 4/4 Time [:15]
42. The D Chord: 3/4 Time [:17]
43. The D Chord: 4/4 Time [:24]
44. Darling Nellie Gray [1:33]
45. My Bonnie [:57]
46. Little Annie Rooney [:55]
47. Oh! Susanna [:44]
48. Good Night Ladies [:48]
49. Moveable Chords, 7th Chords Outro [2:29]

*This book is available as a book only or as a book/compact disc configuration.

A teaching DVD (93260DVD) of the music in this book is now available. The publisher strongly recommends the use this resource along with the text to insure accuracy of interpretation and ease in learning.

1 2 3 4 5 6 7 8 9 0

© 1962 BY MEL BAY PUBLICATIONS, INC., PACIFIC, MO 63069.
ALL RIGHTS RESERVED. INTERNATIONAL COPYRIGHT SECURED. B.M.I. MADE AND PRINTED IN U.S.A.
No part of this publication may be reproduced in whole or in part, or stored in a retrieval system, or transmitted in any form or by any means, electronic, mechanical, photocopy, recording, or otherwise, without written permission of the publisher.

Visit us on the Web at www.melbay.com — E-mail us at email@melbay.com

Tuning the Tenor Banjo

First String . . . . A ①
Second String . . . . D ②
Third String . . . . G ③
Fourth String . . . . C ④

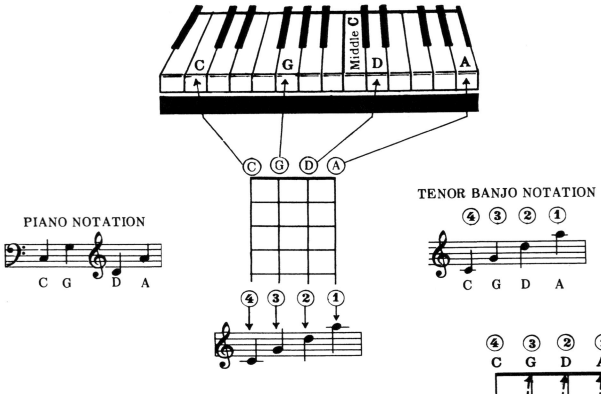

PIANO NOTATION

TENOR BANJO NOTATION

ANOTHER METHOD OF TUNING

PLACE THE FINGER BEHIND THE SEVENTH FRET OF THE FOURTH STRING TO OBTAIN THE PITCH OF THE THIRD STRING (G).

PLACE THE FINGER BEHIND THE SEVENTH FRET OF THE THIRD STRING TO OBTAIN THE PITCH OF THE SECOND STRING (D).

PLACE THE FINGER BEHIND THE SEVENTH FRET OF THE SECOND STRING TO OBTAIN THE PITCH OF THE FIRST STRING (A).

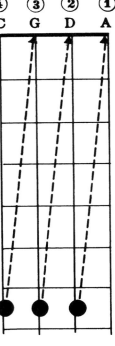

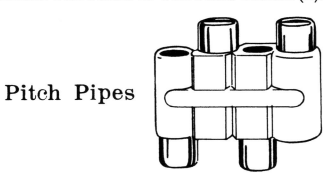

Pitch Pipes

PITCH PIPES FOR THE TENOR BANJO (CELLO) MAY BE PURCHASED AT ANY MUSIC STORE. EACH PIPE WILL HAVE THE CORRECT PITCH OF EACH TENOR BANJO STRING. THESE ARE AN EXCELLENT INVESTMENT.

THE CORRECT WAY TO HOLD THE TENOR BANJO

THIS IS THE PICK

Hold it in this manner ⟶ firmly between the thumb and first finger. Use a medium soft pick.

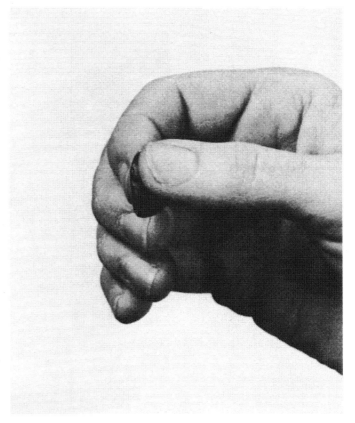

THE LEFT HAND

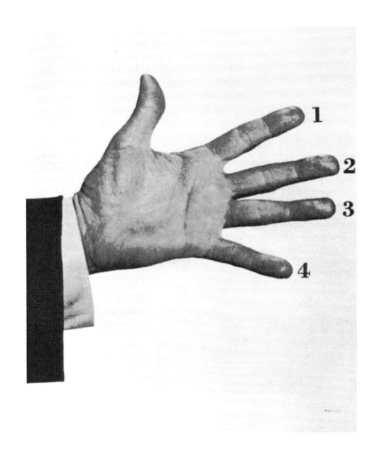

Practice holding the Tenor Banjo in this manner.

Keep the palm of the hand away from the neck of the instrument.

THE FINGERBOARD

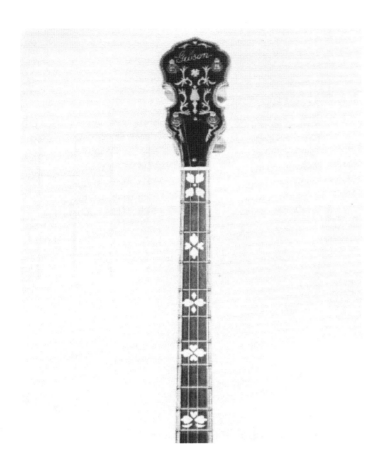

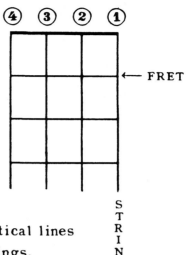

The vertical lines are the strings.

The horizontal lines are the frets.

The encircled numbers are the number of the strings.

Striking the Strings

⊓ = Down stroke of the pick.

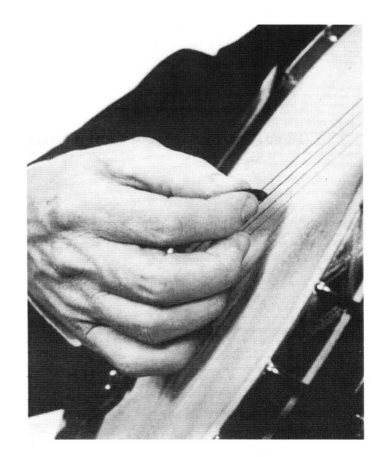

OUR FIRST CHORD

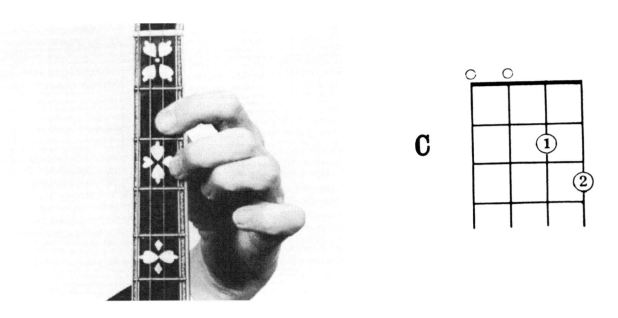

Do not place fingers on the frets but directly behind them.

Do not apply too much pressure.

Practice the above Chord until the tone is clear.

/ / / / = Strokes of the Pick over the Strings.

/ / / = Strum the C chord three times in succession.

TIME SIGNATURES

$\frac{4}{4}$ or C = COMMON TIME

Hold the C chord and play it in this manner:

```
     C              C              C              C
4/4  / / / /        / / / /        / / / /        / / / /
```

$\frac{3}{4}$ = THREE-FOUR or WALTZ TIME

Hold the C chord and play it in the following manner:

```
     C           C           C           C
3/4  / / /       / / /       / / /       / / /
```

$\frac{2}{4}$ = TWO-FOUR TIME

Play it in this manner:

```
     C
2/4  / /     / /     / /     / /
```

THE G7 CHORD

Play the C and G7 chords in the following manner:

| C | C | G7 | G7 |

$\frac{4}{4}$ / / / /   / / / /   / / / /   / / / /

| C | G7 | C | G7 |

/ / / /   / / / /   / / / /   / / / /

| C | G7 | C | G7 | C | G7 | C |

/ / / /   / / / /   / / / /   / 𝄽 / 𝄽
                                                                 REST

𝄽 = Rest.   It indicates a period of silence.

See "TENOR BANJO CHORDS"
by MEL BAY

OUR FIRST SONG
(Using the C and G7 Chords)

Long, Long Ago

Be sure to play the chords directly on each word or syllable as indicated.

Down In The Valley

* Continue playing the C chord until you reach the G7 chord.
  Play G7 until you arrive at C.

Skip To My Lou

* No chord strokes on words in parenthesis ( ).

Buffalo Gals

Oh, My Darling Clementine

There will be no playing on the pick-up notes
at the beginning of the above song.

*For additional Chords,
See "TENOR BANJO CHORDS"
by MEL BAY*

THE "F" CHORD

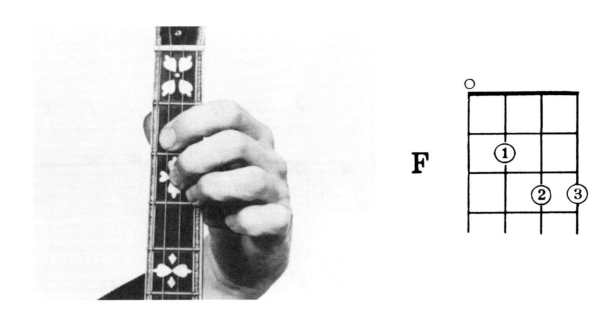

Master the following Chord Study:

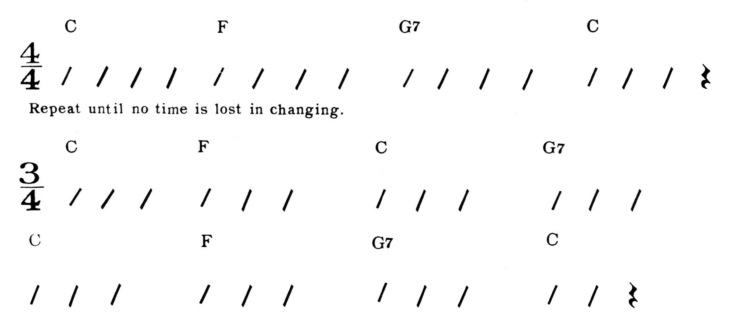

The C, F and G7 chords are the principal chords in the Key of C.

See "TENOR BANJO CHORDS"
by MEL BAY

The Blue Tail Fly

* 𝄐 = Hold the note extra long as in a pause.

**See "TENOR BANJO CHORDS"
by MEL BAY**

The Marines Hymn

There Is A Tavern In The Town

* The Pick-up note may be played by striking the third string open.

THE D7 CHORD

Play the following Chord Study:

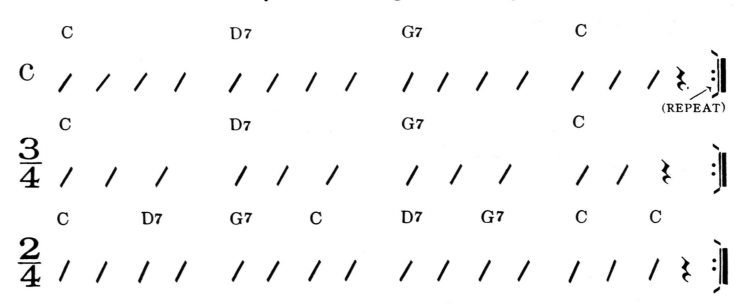

Master the above study before proceeding.

See "TENOR BANJO CHORDS" by MEL BAY

Our Boys Will Shine Tonight
(Introducing the D7 Chord)

In the last measure play the bass note on the first beat,
rest and play the C chord on the third beat.
The fourth beat is silent.

THE G CHORD

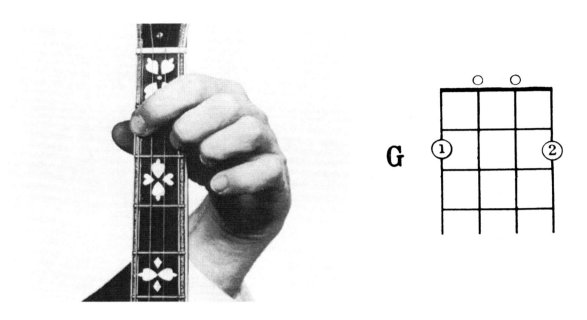

The chords in the Key of G are: G, C and D7.

Play the following Chord Study:

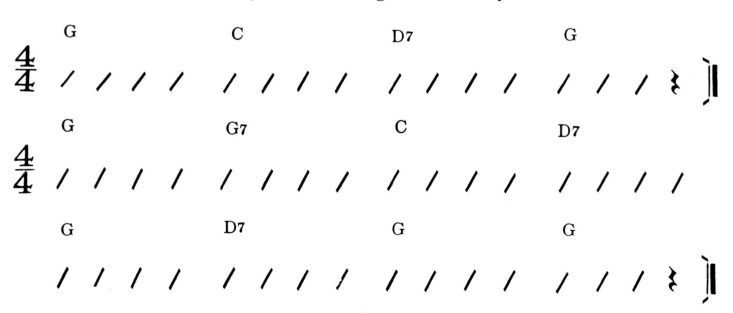

**See TENOR BANJO CHORDS
in PHOTO-DIAGRAM FORM
by MEL BAY**

The Old Grey Mare

She'll Be Coming Round The Mountain

Hand Me Down My Walking Cane

In order to start your song in the correct key,
strum the principal chord lightly before beginning.
In the above song the principal or tonic chord is G.

Red River Valley

SOME MORE CHORDS

 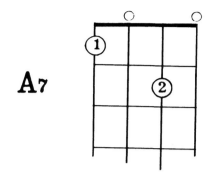

A7

 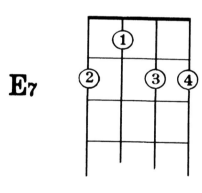

E7

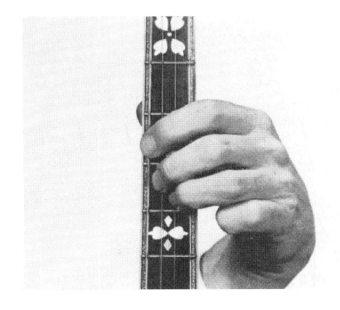 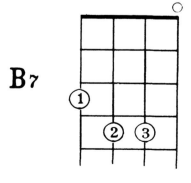

B7

FUN WITH CHORDS IN "C"

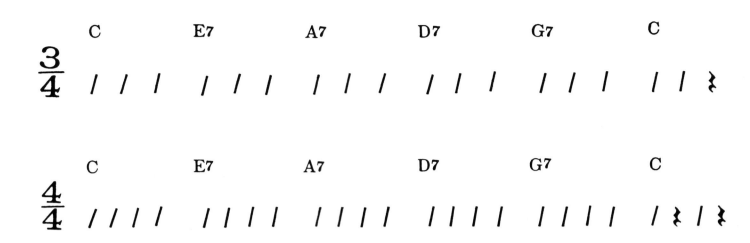

MORE FUN WITH CHORDS IN "G"

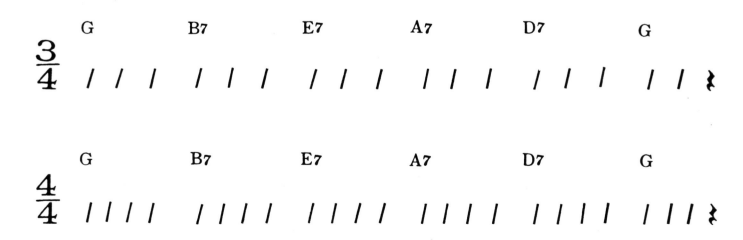

**See "TENOR BANJO CHORDS"
by MEL BAY**

Home on The Range

I've Been Working On The Railroad

In The Evening By The Moonlight

In the above song
strum the chords slowly.

THE D CHORD

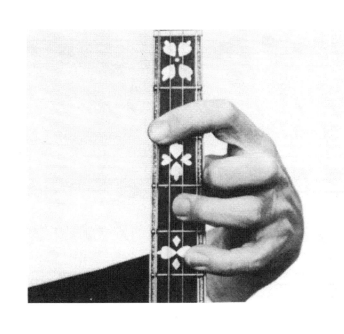

D	G	A7	D

4/4   / / / /   / / / /   / / / /   / / / /

D	G	A7	D

3/4   / / /   / / /   / / /   / / 𝄾

D	B7	E7	A7

4/4   / / / /   / / / /   / / / /   / / / /

D	D7	G	D

/ / / /   / / / /   / / / /   / / / 𝄾

33

Darling Nellie Gray

My Bonnie

Little Annie Rooney

Oh! Susanna

Good Night Ladies

SUMMARY
The Major Chords

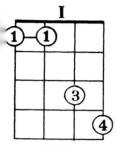

I

Frets	1	2	3	4	5	6	7	8	9	10	11	12
Chords	Db	D	Eb	E	F	F#/Gb	G	Ab	A	Bb	B	C

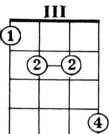

III

Frets	1	2	3	4	5	6	7	8	9	10	11	12
Chords	A	Bb	B	C	Db/C#	D	Eb	E	F	Gb/F#	G	Ab

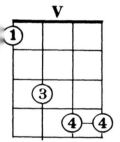

V

Frets	1	2	3	4	5	6	7	8	9	10	11	12
Chords	Gb/F#	G	Ab	A	Bb	B	C	Db/C#	D	Eb	E	F

The Minor Chords

Im

Frets	1	2	3	4	5	6	7	8	9	10	11	12
Chords	Dbm	Dm	Ebm	Em	Fm	Gbm/F#m	Gm	Abm	Am	Bbm	Bm	Cm

IIIm

Frets	1	2	3	4	5	6	7	8	9	10	11	12
Chords	Bbm	Bm	Cm	Dbm/C#m	Dm	Ebm	Em	Fm	Gbm/F#m	Gm	Abm	Am

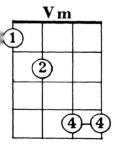

Vm

Frets	1	2	3	4	5	6	7	8	9	10	11	12
Chords	Gbm/F#m	Gm	Abm	Am	Bbm	Bm	Cm	Dbm/C#m	Dm	Ebm	Em	Fm

THE SEVENTH CHORDS

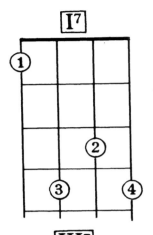

I⁷

Frets	1	2	3	4	5	6	7	8	9	10	11	12
Chords	Db7	D7	Eb7	E7	F7	Gb7 F#7	G7	Ab7	A7	Bb7	B7	C7

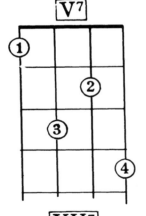

III⁷

Frets	1	2	3	4	5	6	7	8	9	10	11	12
Chords	Ab7	A7	Bb7	B7	C7	Db7 C#7	D7	Eb7	E7	F7	Gb7 F#7	G7

V⁷

Frets	1	2	3	4	5	6	7	8	9	10	11	12
Chords	Gb7 F#7	G7	Ab7	A7	Bb7	B7	C7	Db7 C#7	D7	Eb7	E7	F7

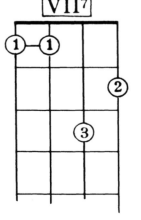

VII⁷

Frets	1	2	3	4	5	6	7	8	9	10	11	12
Chords	Db7	D7	Eb7	E7	F7	Gb7 F#7	G7	Ab7	A7	Bb7	B7	C7

THE ROMAN NUMERAL ABOVE THE FORM INDICATES
THE CHORDAL TONE FOUND ON THE FIRST STRING.